SABBATH SPICE
AND
FESTIVAL FARE

To my daughter
VIOLA REINE
who heard and liked these Talks;
and to all other children
who may be pleased to read them.

SABBATH SPICE and FESTIVAL FARE

SABBATH SPICE
&
FESTIVAL FARE

TALKS TO CHILDREN

By
Dayan Dr. A. FELDMAN

LONDON
GEORGE ROUTLEDGE & SONS, LTD.
BROADWAY HOUSE: 68-74 CARTER LANE, E.C.
1927

Printed in Great Britain by Stephen Austin & Sons, Ltd., Hertford.

CONTENTS

PREFACE

MY interest in the cause of Jewish Education has brought me into frequent touch with our children and our youths, whom I have addressed with great delight both in synagogue and school.

The Talks which comprise this volume are based upon those actually delivered on different occasions. It is hoped that in this new form they will reach and appeal to wider circles.

I have avoided rigid consistency in the transliteration of Hebrew terms into English, keeping in view my youthful readers, for whom the book is intended.

I am indebted to many friends who read these Talks and urged their publication, and more particularly to Mr. H. M. Adler, M.A., LL.M., Mr. G. Costa, Mr. Jack M. Myers, Mr. M. Silvestone, B.A., and Mr. J. H. Taylor, B.A., for helpful suggestions in preparing this volume for the press.

A. F.

TALKS TO CHILDREN

SABBATH SPICE

I wonder whether you have ever read or heard about Hadrian, the Roman Emperor ? He lived in the early part of the second century. Perhaps you know him better as the Roman who once governed Britain. He was active and very inquisitive, and often conversed with Rabbi Joshua ben Chananiah, a witty Jewish sage, whom he asked many puzzling questions. One day, while discussing the Sabbath, he asked the Rabbi, " Why are your Sabbath dishes so tasty ? " Some think that Hadrian did not ask this question merely for information but in a kind of mocking manner ; for the Emperor, like many other Romans of those days, was not at all sympathetic to the Jewish observance of the Sabbath. He did not understand the religious meaning and beauty of this or any other Jewish ceremony. He probably thought that

our Sabbath was merely a day of special
dishes and fine clothes. But the Rabbi was
equal to the task. He met the Emperor's
mockery with a clever and dignified retort.
" There is a certain spice," said he, " which
makes everything we have on our day of
rest specially sweet and pleasant to the taste.
This spice bears the name of ' Sabbath '."

" And where, pray, might it be obtained,
and how can I secure some of it ? " inquired
the Emperor. To which the Rabbi replied :
" It would not be of much good to you if
you did obtain it, for this spice is rather
unusual in that it spreads its sweetness
only when used by people who observe the
seventh day as holy. When handled by people
who do not care to do so, it loses these
qualities altogether."

This was a fine reply and served as a lesson.
It meant to convey to Jews, and also to people
who are not Jews, that the beauty and charm
of our sacred Sabbath becomes real to those
alone who treat it with respect and observe
it with love. In the prayers for the Sabbath
are the words : " They that find delight in

it shall inherit glory for everlasting ; they that taste it are worthy of life."

Here is another poetic gem about the Sabbath. You remember reading in the first chapter of the Bible that God breathed into man the breath of life, which means God gave man the gift of a soul. This soul, this breath of life within us, helps us to feel, to think, and to act. Now our Rabbis loved to tell the following pretty story : On the eve of the Sabbath, another soul, besides the one we have with us throughout the week, wings its way from on high and enters our bodies. It remains with us during the whole of the Day of Rest. It raises our spirits, stimulates our desire for reading, for study, and prayer, and increases our feelings of happiness and joy. When Sabbath ends and the prayer called *Havdoloh* (הַבְדָּלָה) is recited, this welcome guest of ours, the added soul, takes to itself wings and returns to its shelter beneath the Throne of God where it waits to revisit us on the following Sabbath eve.

Some people see this pretty story in the

kindling of the Sabbath lights. As you know, two candles are lit in the Jewish home at the incoming of the Sabbath. Why two? Here is the reason usually given :

The two lights remind us of the *two* forms in which the command about the Sabbath was given us. In the Book of Exodus, the Fourth Commandment reads : " *Remember* the Sabbath day to keep it holy," whilst in Deuteronomy, the same Commandment says : " *Observe* the Sabbath day to keep it holy."

But here is another suggested reason for the two Sabbath lights. " Light " in the Bible often means " Soul ". " The soul of man is the light of God ", we read in the Book of Proverbs. The two Sabbath lights, therefore, stand for the *two souls* ; that is the ordinary soul and the additional, the Sabbath soul.

This pretty thought does not end here. In the *Havdoloh* ceremony, at the going out of the Sabbath, we use, in addition to wine and light, some sweet-smelling spices, called *Besomim* (בְּשָׂמִים). Now, why do we use spices? " Ah," say our poetic sages, " Does not the

added soul leave us just at this hour and
so make us feel sad ? The spices, with their
refreshing sweetness, are therefore taken
to cheer our drooping spirits at the leave-
taking of this cherished guest."

The Rabbis have told us these two pretty
fancies of the Sabbath spice and the added
soul for a special reason. They wanted to
express the wonderful effect that the Sabbath
day produces upon people who observe it
to keep it holy. Rightly kept, the Jewish
Sabbath spreads an air of charm and cheer
in Jewish homes and hearts. In the Bible
and in the Prayer Book the Sabbath is
called the "desirable of days", a "pleasurable
delight". Our Rabbis and poets have called
it "The Bride", "The Queen", "The
Princess".

Look up the Prayer Book and you will
find these pretty words and phrases in our
Sabbath prayers and songs. For example,
"Come my beloved to meet the bride, let
us welcome the Sabbath tide", is the oft-
repeated chant of the *Lecho Dodi* (לְכָה דוֹדִי)
on Friday night.

The Sabbath brings us festivity and
happiness as if it were a bride. It invests
the home with a queenly dignity and grace.
There is nothing so exquisitely beautiful
as the real Jewish Friday night and
Sabbath day at home, with the table decked,
the lights kindled, the grace sung, the rest-
fulness enjoyed. As " Bride ", " Princess ",
and " Queen " the Sabbath has been honoured
in poetry and song, and especially in the
Sabbath Table hymns, called in Hebrew
Zemiros (זְמִירוֹת).

These *Zemiros* give life to the ideas and
fancies which our Rabbis have woven around
the Added Soul and the Sabbath Spice,
and they help to create the Sabbath feeling
which makes the home aglow with light
and joy.

ABRAHAM'S CHARM

GREAT was the interest taken in the Jewish
Exhibition organized at the Art Gallery
in East London. It was visited by large
crowds from all parts of London and also
from the Provinces. The Exhibition con-
sisted of a variety of objects, coming from
different places and belonging to different
periods. It provided an " illustrated guide "
to Jewish thought, and supplied picturesque
and fascinating helps to the study of the
history and literature of our people. Among
the most attractive exhibits was a beautiful
collection of antique charms. Displayed
in one of the show cases, they drew considerable
attention.

You know, of course, what charms are.
They are made of different metals, like gold,
and silver, and of precious stones ; they are
varied in shape, design, and inscription.
They were worn by our people, at different
periods and in different lands, on their

fingers and around their necks ; and, like
all charms, were believed to possess very
special powers.

Now, why should I mention just this
section when all the objects exhibited were
of such wonderful fascination ? It is because
I would like to direct your attention to one
particular Jewish charm of very, very great
antiquity. It was not shown at this local
Exhibition, nor was it even among the
exhibits of the much larger Anglo-Jewish
Exhibition held at the Royal Albert Hall
many years ago.

This unique charm is said to have been
worn by the Patriarch Abraham, and may
therefore be called " Abraham's charm ".
According to the Rabbis it is mentioned
in the Book of Genesis, in the story of the
life of Abraham. " The Lord," we read
in that Book, " blessed Abraham with everything." " Now," ask the Rabbis, " of what
did this full blessing of Abraham consist ? "
and they proceed to give the reply. Abraham,
they say, was blessed by being the proud
possessor of a charm. According to some

he wore it upon his heart; according to others around his neck. This charm was very remarkable and had peculiar properties.

By means of it Abraham drew unto himself all the kings and princes from the east and west; by its magic power he healed the sick and soothed the ailing: surely a most wonderful charm! What a valuable curio it would have made at any exhibition! It would have attracted once again kings and princes from east and west. In healing power it would have surpassed the most famous and greatest of remedies.

But, of course—you have probably guessed by now—the Rabbis were only speaking in parable; they gave play to a poetic fancy. For Abraham's charm was really not an ordinary jewel worn around his neck, or a mere precious pendant hanging on his breast. The charm was of finer form and more skilful craftsmanship. But it was not something fashioned with the hand. The charm lay in the gentle and soothing words which flowed from his mouth; in the generous feelings of his warm heart. It was Abraham's thoughtfulness and kindly feelings which drew unto himself not alone ordinary people but also kings and rulers, which won for him the love and sympathy of the small as well as the great in the land. It was Abraham's words and Abraham's deeds that healed the sick and consoled the sorrowful, that spread rays of sunshine, of joy, and comfort into many a home and many a heart. This was Abraham's charm of which the Rabbis loved to speak. This was the magic amulet possessed by the first Patriarch.

Such a charm, such an amulet, all children can acquire. Such a precious possession is within the reach of all. It can be obtained through following the advice of parents, teachers, and friends. It can be won by an earnest study of Torah, of Jewish teachings, and by a life lived in accordance with those teachings. The wise King Solomon, in the Book of Proverbs, tells of this kind of charm, and bids us make it our own. " My son," he says, " keep the commandment of thy father and forsake not the teaching of thy mother. *Bind them continually upon thy heart, tie them about thy neck.* . . . My son, keep my words, and lay up my commandments with thee. Keep my commandments and live, and my teaching as the apple of thine eye. *Bind them upon thy fingers, write them upon the table of thy heart.*" The Torah teaches us to be kind. It teaches us to be truthful. It teaches us to shed light over all our surroundings. There will be a sweetness in our words and deeds, in our actions and lives ; a charm as rare and precious as the charm possessed by our father Abraham whom " the Lord blessed with everything ".

THE NEW TERM ✳

WHAT hustle and excitement there was when the school bells rang out that morning.

You ask what morning and why ?

It was the beginning of a new term. Children hurried to school at an early hour. Teachers and pupils were pleased to meet again. They exchanged friendly greetings, and wished each other success during the coming session. New exercise books were made ready, fresh note-books prepared. The children who had done well during the previous term resolved to repeat their triumphs, whilst others who had done badly made up their minds to improve and win through. All eyes turned to the new register at the teacher's desk ; or perhaps it was only the old one, but with a new leaf turned over. There it was, ready to record the attendance, conduct, and work of each one during the term that was just commencing.

12

✳ From Sabbath pure and Holiday Fare by Dayan Dr A Feldman with acknowledgements to the author and Publisher

Rosh Hashonoh (רֹאשׁ הַשָּׁנָה), the beginning of the New Year, is something like the beginning of a new school term.

It is true that there is no ringing of bells, but you do hear, instead, the sound of the *Shofar* (שׁוֹפָר). It is a much more thrilling sound. What peculiar notes, and what a strange variety! There is the long drawn-out sound—the *Tekioh*; there are the triple, broken notes—the *Shevorim*; and there are the thrills of wailing—the *Teruoh*. They seem so full of mystery and awe.

And there is something else.

When you hear the school bell ringing in the new term and calling you to work, it is mainly the sound that attracts you. You hardly think of the bell itself which produces the sound. How different is it with the Shofar which announces Rosh Hashonoh and calls you to fresh effort during that other new term, the New Year.

There is something in the Shofar itself, quite apart from its sound, which stirs the imagination.

Although it is generally translated "trumpet", the Shofar is really not a trumpet in the ordinary sense. It is a plain, almost crude kind of instrument; in fact, it is a ram's horn, and its natural shape is not altered. The custom of blowing it is very, very old. Around it cluster many sacred Jewish memories. You wonder why it is made from a ram's horn. It recalls the *Akedoh* (עֲקֵדָה), the binding of Isaac by his father on Mount Moriah, an event which is said to have happened on Rosh Hashonoh. Of course, you remember the story of the ram caught in the thicket by its horns, and offered up by Abraham in place of Isaac, his son. We read that story from the Scroll of the Law on New Year's Day and refer to it over and over again in our prayers. Again, the blowing of the Shofar recalls the Giving of the Law on Mount Sinai. You will remember the description of that great event in the Bible, where we read, "There were thunders and lightnings and a thick cloud upon the Mount, and the voice of the Shofar exceeding loud."

The Shofar, like the trumpet or bugle nowadays, was used also to assemble the Israelites in their journeyings towards the Holy Land, to get them into proper formation, in military manner, and prepare for battle against their enemies. The same old Shofar, our prophets tell us, will be used to announce the coming of the Messiah, when Israel's exiles will be gathered from the four corners of the earth, when all nations will become happy and free, and when God will be proclaimed Sovereign King of the whole world. You will find all these thoughts about the Shofar in the prayers for the New Year.

So, when the Shofar is used to announce the New Year, even as the school bell that rings in the new term, it should set your mind thinking and recalling; for this is just what you are meant to do on Rosh Hashonoh, the Festival called *Yom Hazzikoron* (יוֹם הַזִּכָּרוֹן) — " The Day of Remembrance." And when you think and remember, you cannot help making up your mind to put forth a great effort in the New Year.

The Shofar reminds you of the *Akedoh*—of Sacrifice ; and so you are urged to make some sacrifices, to give up some of your pleasures and comforts in order to give pleasure and comfort to others.

The Shofar reminds you of the battles of our people against their enemies ; and so you are urged to show fight against different kinds of enemies, against temptation and sin, evil thoughts and evil deeds, which are among the greatest of your foes.

And when the Shofar brings before you pictures of the great and happy future for our people and for everyone else, it urges you to help to bring about that good and glorious time.

If you resolve to do all these things in the New Year, you are sure to receive a good mark in the new Register which is opened up on Rosh Hashonoh, and in which everybody's record is carefully noted.

You have not seen that Register, have you ? But you must have heard or read about it. Have you heard the saying of the Rabbis that three books—three registers—are opened

up on New Year's Day in which are recorded
the reports of three different classes of people
—the good, the bad, and the doubtful ones ?
Possibly you will remember better that
grand and beautiful prayer in the New Year's
service, which speaks about the New Year
Register. This is how it begins : " And we
shall tell of the mighty holiness of this day."
In Synagogue this prayer is read aloud by
all the congregation in a most solemn manner,
and then repeated by the Reader and choir.
There is a pathetic story about this prayer
and how it came to be written. There was
once a great Rabbi, named Rabbi Amnon,
who lived in Mayence many hundred years
ago. The Archbishop of that city tried very
often to persuade him to change his faith.
He, of course, refused ; and the cruel and
angry Archbishop ordered that the Rabbi's
hands and feet should be cut off. Rosh
Hashonoh was then at hand, and the suffering
Rabbi begged to be carried to the Synagogue.
His request was granted. As he entered
the House of Prayer, the Reader was
just preparing to recite the *Kedushoh.*

c

Rabbi Amnon beckoned him to stop, and uttered this prayer which he himself composed: " And we shall tell of the holiness of this day, for it is awe-inspiring. . . . Thou, O God, art the Judge. . . . Thou openest the records, the seal of every man's hand is there. On New Year's Day the inscribing begins, and according to the records, it is decided who shall win the prizes of life, of happiness and joy, and who shall lose all claim to such gifts." When he had finished reciting this prayer, Rabbi Amnon breathed his last and passed away peacefully, a martyr for his faith.

In this New Year's Register, kept by God, the Great Master and Teacher, each one of us has a page, and in that page are entered our conduct and deeds, our marks and our prizes.

What do we wish each other on Rosh Hashonoh ? *Leshonoh Tovoh Tikosevu* (לְשָׁנָה טוֹבָה תִּכָּתֵבוּ), " May you be written down for a good year ! " Again, in the New Year's prayers we ask God repeatedly, " Write us down in the book of life, blessing and peace." Now you know the meaning of these wishes and these prayers ; and I am sure you will, during the New Year, try to act in such a manner as to earn a good mark and win the coveted prizes awarded by God.

ACCORDING TO THE LABOUR IS THE REWARD

CHILDREN delight in mottoes and proverbs and often enjoy writing an essay or composition on such sayings as " The early bird catches the worm ", " Make hay while the sun shines ", " Strike the iron while it is hot ". Jewish children will therefore be pleased to learn that there is a most interesting collection of Jewish sayings in the Hebrew Prayer Book. Its orginal place is in the Talmud. It is called the " Ethics of the Fathers " פִּרְקֵי אָבוֹת. It collects many teachings of the Jewish Sages of old.

This collection is divided into six chapters. Of these we read one every Sabbath afternoon during the spring and summer, between Pesach and Rosh Hashonoh, and repeat the whole series each six weeks.

Let me paraphrase two or three of these sayings which deal especially with children, and may interest you.

Here is one : " It is always safer to keep quiet," says a Jewish Rabbi, " for whoever talks much in season and out of season makes mischief and gets into trouble." What an excellent subject is this for a composition—rather like the proverb, " Silence is golden."

Here is a second : " The bashful pupil will not learn." This means that those who are ashamed to ask for an explanation of what they do not understand will make no progress in their work. This is something which school-children should always bear in mind.

And there is one more : " Whatever one learns as a child is well preserved, like an exercise written with ink on clean paper." This warns us that children with their clear and fresh minds ought to be especially accurate in their studies. For whatever they learn in their youth clings to their memory and cannot be rubbed off.

These are just three specimen sayings. But there are many other such " wise saws " in that famous collection, the " Ethics of the Fathers ". I should advise you to dip into it in your spare time.

Here I propose to deal more fully with one of them. It is the last saying in the fifth chapter. It consists of three words : לְפוּם צַעֲרָא אַגְרָא. Translated into English it means, " According to the labour is the reward."

There is an interesting story told about one who, in the early years of his life, was a shepherd. He had never studied and of course knew nothing either of Hebrew or any other subject. Once upon a time—he was already getting on in years—he came to a well to draw water. He noticed close to this well a hard rock with a large hole in it. He began to wonder how this came about. The people who stood around, seeing his surprise, said in explanation, " Every day drops of water keep falling on to this rock, and so regularly and repeatedly do they strike it that they have worn this hole into it." " Surely," said the ignorant shepherd to himself, " if this hard rock could be affected by these persistent drops

of water, my mind, which I hope is not quite
as hard as stone, can be affected by continuous
study." He went away and applied himself
to his work with all his might. He started
with the *Aleph Beth*. He worked on steadily,
and his labours were rewarded. He made
excellent progress, and this ignorant shepherd
became one of the greatest Rabbis we have
had. His name is Rabbi Akiba.

Of course, not all children are blessed with
the same powers of mind. The naturally
clever and gifted children are the exception ;
but no child, not even the dullest, need despair
of success. It is not always the clever children
that are the most successful. It is rather
the steady, painstaking, persevering ones
that get on well at school. It is the industrious
that win the greater success in later life.
Not according to the measure of cleverness,
but " according to the *labour* "—the toil, the
pains taken—" is the reward."

Most of you have learned geography at
school, and know something about the course
of rivers and the flow of waters. Where do
rivers rise ? In the mountains. But do

they remain in the high places ? No. They
run down and seek a level in the sea. A
Jewish sage, thinking of this peculiarity of
water, said : " Knowledge is like unto water.
For just as water leaves a high level and
remains in a low one, so does knowledge
desert those who think too highly of themselves, and it clings to those who are lowly
in their own opinion and therefore continue
to work steadily and to study diligently."
Their work is rewarded. For " according
to the labour is their reward."

It is a striking fact that many children
who in their early youth were exceptionally
bright and clever often fail to realize the
hopes of their parents and teachers. For these
very clever children become so conceited
and over-confident that they will do no work,
imagining that knowledge will fly into their
clever little heads without any effort of their
own. Let those who are blessed with excep-
tional intelligence and ability bear this in
mind. Let them remember that, with all
their cleverness, they must continue their work.
For " according to the *labour* is the reward."

Now apart from study and work in school, there is yet another way in which this saying might be of help to children. There are some who, having fallen into bad habits, lose heart. They begin to think that their faults are beyond remedy, and in a despairing mood continue in their evil ways. If there are any such children, they must try their hardest to free themselves from these habits, and be sure that success will crown their efforts. A Jewish wise man once said : " If anyone tells you I have tried and have not succeeded, do not believe him." Probably he has not tried hard enough. For according to the effort is the measure of success : " According to the labour is the reward."

The story is told of a man who had proceeded so very far in the path of wrong that he began to feel as if all hope for him was gone. God was angry with him. In his despair he wandered among the mountains and hills. " Oh ye mountains ! Oh ye hills ! " he exclaimed, " Ask for mercy on my behalf." But the mountains stood still. They could do nothing for him. He asked of the moon and the stars to help him. But they, too, remained silent. Then, he reflected : " Why should not I myself try ? Surely the remedy lies in my own hand rather than with anyone else." At that moment, so the story goes, tears came into his eyes. His evil nature took a turn for the better. And so complete, so wonderful was the change, that he heard a voice, as from heaven, exclaim : " This man, having so completely mended his ways, has deserved the blessings of Almighty God." His own efforts saved him. " According to his labour was the reward."

At school, the reward for good conduct and progress comes regularly, in visible and welcome form. It takes the shape of books or other gifts on Prize Day. In life, too, the reward for good conduct and good work does come in the end, although it does not always come so soon or so regularly. But there is also a higher and richer kind of reward which always follows the doing of a good action. It is the pleasure, the satisfaction, the joy of having done it, the feeling that our character has been made stronger, our nature nobler, and our soul purer by the performance of a worthy deed. As a Jewish Rabbi beautifully expressed it in the same collection of the Ethics of the Fathers: *Sechar Mitzvoh Mitzvoh* (שְׂכַר מִצְוָה מִצְוָה). The reward of a good deed is the fact that we have done it. For one good deed gives us power to do yet another, and that power is part of our reward.

Added to this is the knowledge that our good actions will be pleasing to our Father in Heaven, that they will merit and receive His reward. This world is a garden. We are all workers in the garden. Our Master is God. And as the Rabbis again tell us in the Ethics of the Fathers: "The Employer will surely pay the reward of our labour."

SUCCOS MESSAGES

A MAN was once asked which of the three great Jewish Festivals he liked best. " Shovuos (The Feast of Weeks)," he replied ; and he proceeded to give his reasons. " On Pesach (the Feast of Unleavened Bread)," said he, " we cannot eat whatever we like, although we may eat wherever we like. On Succos (the Feast of Tabernacles), again, we may eat whatever we like, but cannot eat wherever we like. On Shovuos, however, we can eat whatever we like (provided, of course, it is Kosher) and wherever we like."

Children, I am sure, like all Festivals equally well. And the reason of this is not far to seek. In the first place, all Festivals mean holidays from school—much play and no work ; and you must enjoy an occasional break from school. But quite apart from this fact, there is in every one of the three Festivals something special that is interesting and appealing to young folks.

On Passover, there is, of course, the Seder Service, with its peculiar charm for children.

On the Feast of Weeks, there are the flowers and plants in the Synagogues : objects of special delight to children, who are extremely fond of beautiful Nature. Whilst on the Feast of Tabernacles, there are several ceremonies and observances in Synagogue and home, which must cheer the hearts and please the minds of our little friends.

First, there is the Succah. And how children love the Succah ! Long before the coming of the Festival, boys and girls look forward to the pleasure of helping their parents to make and to decorate the little hut ; and during the Festival itself they love to go the round of as many Succahs as possible to admire the tasteful decorations, and no doubt also to enjoy some of the dainties provided in them.

And people are delighted to welcome these little visitors in their Succahs. There is a pretty prayer which some people recite every day as they enter the Succah. It is in the form of an invitation and begins, " Enter

ye guests ! " In this prayer we ask the
spirits of the past—Abraham, Isaac, Jacob,
Joseph, Moses, Aaron, and David—to enter
in turn and hover in "our tabernacle of peace."
With these ancient guests of the past who
are with us in spirit, we like to have, in the
flesh, the cheery youthful visitors—the boys
and girls—who are growing up, and who
some day will make and dwell in Succahs
of their own ; and in their turn invite the
younger people of their generation to join
them as welcome visitors.

Besides the Succah, there are the ceremonies
in the Synagogue itself. Can you recall
some of them ? There is, first of all, the
" waving of the palms "; then the procession,
once each day of the Festival (except on
Sabbath), and seven times on the seventh
day, called Hoshano Rabboh. On Simchas
Torah, which is the last day of the Festival,
there is a "procession" of the Scrolls. Every
one on that day is called to the Reading of
the Law, and with what delight boys rush
along with others to the Almemar to take
part in the "calling-up" to the Law, and the

distribution of sweets which, in some congregations, follows this " calling-up ".

All these events are pleasant and delightful.

Now if there is in every Festival so much to entertain and to please children, there is also a great deal to interest and to instruct them.

Every Jewish Festival has its object-lessons, and wise children who keep open their eyes, ears, and minds to these messages, will grow wiser and better with every Festival, as it passes by.

What are the lessons that children may learn from the Feast of Tabernacles ? They are centred in the two chief ceremonies and observances of this Festival : the Succah, and the Four Plants, both of which supply enjoyable teaching in poetic form for girls and boys.

The Succah, the small rustic hut in which we are told to dwell for seven days, carries our minds back to Israel's childhood and youth. It recalls the early period in the life of the Jewish people, from the time they left Egypt to become a nation to the time they entered and settled in the Promised Land.

What, according to Jewish Law, is needed in the making of a proper Succah, so that it may become a worthy reminder of Israel's childhood and youth ?

The Succah, our Rabbis tell us, must be made very beautiful. It is a Mitzvoh (a religious duty) to decorate and adorn it as much as possible. Yet with all this, it must be simple and natural. Again, although the Succah building—the walls—need not be over-elaborate, or over-strong, yet it should be sufficiently firm and steady, so that a passing wind shall not shake or move the Succah, or put out the lights that are kindled within it.

Moreover, the Succah (סֻכָּה) proper, that is the *Sechach* (סְכָךְ), the covering on the roof, must be free from any substance or material which can become unclean and impure. These are among the main properties of a Kosher Succah. Now the Succah, as you have already been told, is a reminder of the childhood and youth of our people.

It must be a pattern for your childhood and youth. Your childhood, your youth, must be fashioned after the manner of the Succah. It should be comely and beautiful, yet simple and natural; steady and secure against the winds of passing fancies; free from unclean thoughts and actions.

Lessons of equal importance are taught by the second observance of the Succos Festival: The taking of the *Lulov* (לוּלָב), the *Esrog* (אֶתְרוֹג), the *Hadassim* (הֲדַסִּים), the *Arovos* (עֲרָבוֹת). A Jewish Rabbi of long ago once gave an object lesson on the four plants. He pointed out their resemblance to the parts of the human body, as follows :—

"Look at the Lulov, the palm-branch," said he, "with the leaves issuing from the trunk. How strikingly like the human frame!" "Now," he continued, "the Lulov must be perfectly straight and upright; even so must our behaviour and conduct be upright and straight.

"The Esrog is in shape like the human heart. Now, the Esrog, according to the

D

Law, must be flawless, stainless, and perfect ; even so must our heart be without a flaw, perfect and pure.

" The Hadassim, the myrtles, with their small, almond-shaped leaves, resemble the human eye. Now the myrtle stands for kindliness and gentleness ; even so must our outlook be kindly and gentle.

" The longer but narrower leaves of the willows of the brook, have the appearance of the human mouth. Now the willows, growing by the riverside, draw their nurture from its refreshing waters ; even so must our mouths drink deep of the waters of the Torah."

These are some of the thoughts which flow from the observances of this Festival, from the Succah and the Four Plants.

They urge you to spend the period of your youth profitably and well, and so make your lives, like the Feast of Tabernacles, " a Season of Joy."

HAPPY OUR YOUTH

"Happy is our youth, for it has not disgraced our old age." This is a refrain from a song preserved to us from the days of old, and is found in the Talmud.

It was recited or sung in the time of the Temple, nearly two thousand years ago, by a band of good and pious people during *Simchas Bes-Hashoevoh* (שִׂמְחַת בֵּית הַשּׁוֹאֵבָה), the special "Rejoicings at the Drawing of the Waters" connected with the Feast of Tabernacles.

In those early days the Festival of Succos was much more a "Season of Rejoicing" than it is now. In some places, it is still so even at the present time.

Let me just describe to you the kind of festivities that took place in olden times in Jerusalem, during the week of Succos. On the second night of the Festival, the Court of the Temple was most brilliantly illuminated. A beautiful effect was obtained by means of four golden oil-lamps of tremendous size, which were set up on very high pedestals, and were reached by long ladders.

I need not say who climbed those ladders to do the lighting up. Lads of course; the boy-priests in training. They enjoyed doing those things then, as you would have done, and their elders were delighted to give them the opportunity of taking part in the service and encouraging their interest in it. The light produced by these four lamps was most powerful. The flames seemed like a sea of fire. They lit up every nook and corner of the large city of Jerusalem, so that the women could do their needlework in their private enclosures or gardens without the help of any additional light.

Vast were the crowds that assembled in the Temple Court. The ladies were accommodated in galleries, just as in our Synagogues; whilst the men and, of course, the boys crowded in the area below, making as merry as they could and indulging in all sorts of amusement.

The Levites' choir sang and played. The

people who could not sing well or had no instruments shouted and clapped their hands. Everybody helped to make it an occasion of real rejoicing.

The Rabbis also took part in the proceedings. It is recorded in the Talmud, that one of the Rabbis amused the people by juggling with eight lighted torches, throwing them into the air and catching them again; whilst another performed acrobatic exercises that might have gained the prize in any athletic competition.

You see, these Rabbis, who were great scholars but at the same time very human, acted upon the advice of Koheleth or Ecclesiastes, the great Preacher (whose book is read on the Sabbath during the week of Succos) who says : " There is a season for everything, and a time for every purpose under the heavens "—a time for study, and a time for play ; a time for serious work, and a time for recreation.

It was during those Succos celebrations of old, in the course of those far away rejoicings, that the good and pious people

danced and sang with torches in their hands.
They sang sacred hymns and composed
clever proverbs. One of them was the saying
quoted above : "Happy is our youth
(אַשְׁרֵי יַלְדוּתֵנוּ), for it has not disgraced our
old age."

What was the meaning of the verse, it
may be asked, and why was it sung just then ?
We can guess the reason. The singing and
the dancing, the glee and the merrymaking
must have reminded these Rabbis of the
days of their childhood ; for we are all jollier
when we are young. As these older men
looked back upon the early years of their
life, they were delighted to think that
throughout the years of their youth, they had
done nothing to regret or to be ashamed
of in later life. "Happy is our youth," they
shouted with joy, " it has not disgraced our
advanced years."

It was a most happy idea to sing such a
verse at a time when young people were
present in such large numbers. It was an
excellent opportunity to teach the younger
generation, and to impress upon them the

lesson that at no time in their youth, not even in the excitement of play, or in the enthusiasm of a game, must they forget themselves ; at no moment in their childhood or youth must they do anything which they might repent at leisure, when they are older and more sensible ; nothing which might shame them, their parents, their race, or their faith.

And it is a refrain which children may well learn by heart and ever try to remember. Happy is the period of youth of which one has no cause to be ashamed in later life.

Have you ever watched the growth of trees and plants ? Have you noticed how some trees grow up straight, stately, and beautiful, whilst others are crooked, bent, and ugly ? Why is this ? It depends very largely on whether these trees have been looked after and taken proper care of, when still young, tender, and flexible. And children are like trees. This is why so much care and attention, so much labour and pain, are bestowed upon children of school age.

Every school has its system of inspection by doctors who look after the bodily health of the children, just as they have teachers to look after their school training. For "The child is father to the man", and "Youth must be trained in the way it should go, so that it turn not away from it when it grows old".

Parents and teachers do their share of the training. It is for you children to show yourselves ready and willing to be trained; so that when you have grown into men and women, you can say, as did the good and pious people of old: "Happy was our youth, it has not made us feel ashamed of it now when we have grown older." Something more. Your youth misspent or wasted does not injure you alone. It brings discredit and shame also upon your elders, your parents and teachers. It even affects the good name of your people and your faith.

It is related in Jewish history that in olden times, when an enemy marched against Jerusalem and was about to launch an attack upon the city, he would first capture some of the children from the town and inquire what they had done in school that day, what lesson they had been taught. "Tell me the text of your lesson," would be the question put to them. And it depended very much upon the answers given by those children, whether the enemy proceeded with his attack or gave up his plans. For the ways and the manners, the speech and the replies of the children served to show the state of the town, and the condition of its inhabitants. Thus these school children would often be the cause of bringing either relief or ruin upon the whole town and its people.

It is so even now. By their habits and their ways, by their conduct and their actions Jewish children bring either honour or shame upon the Jewish people.

The lesson is clear. You girls and boys must learn to use well the period of your childhood, the years of your youth, so that when you have grown older you may recall those days without any sorrow and regret, but rather, in a spirit of satisfaction and joy, repeat the refrain of the ancient Succos song, "Happy is our youth, for it has not disgraced our old age."

ACCORDING TO PLAN

THE first Sabbath after Succos is known as *Shabbas Bereshis* (שַׁבַּת בְּרֵאשִׁית), the "Sabbath of Creation". *Bereshis* is the first word of the first *Sidrah,* or weekly portion of the *Chumesh* or Pentateuch. It tells the story of the creation of the world. As you probably know, we read one Sidrah— very rarely two—each Sabbath. We also read a portion from the Prophets, which we call the *Haphtorah.* The reading of the whole Torah is completed once each year on the last day of Succos, which is therefore called Simchas Torah, " The Day of Rejoicing in the Law."

The " Sabbath of Creation " thus follows closely upon " The Day of Rejoicing in the Law " ; and our Rabbis saw a pretty idea in this close connection of the two. They put it in the form of a parable taken from the building industry.

42

I wonder if you know much about house-building or town-planning.

Everyone will tell you that, before a house or a town is built up, proper plans are prepared and designs drawn up by an architect. These plans and designs set out in detail all the features of the proposed building. They are constantly consulted by the builder, and serve him as a guide in his work.

God, say the Rabbis, speaking in parable, is a Master-builder. He created the Universe, and, in carrying out the work, He consulted a book of plans and designs which He had by Him from ancient days. It was His own book of plans, for God was also the Architect and Surveyor as well as the Builder of the Universe. This book is none other than the Torah which He handed to Israel and Mankind from the heights of Sinai. With its aid He fashioned the World. "But whence did the Rabbis get this fanciful idea?" you will ask. They found it in the Book of Proverbs—one of the Wisdom Books of the Bible, and attributed to the wise king Solomon. In that Book, Wisdom or the

Torah (for the Torah is Wisdom), appeals
for our respect and acceptance.

> Receive my instruction, and not silver ;
> And knowledge rather than choice gold.

To strengthen this appeal, Wisdom or the
Torah boasts of its hoary antiquity and of
its earliest association with God Himself,
the Source of all Wisdom. This is what
it says :—

> The Lord made me "as the beginning" (*Reshis*, רֵאשִׁית)
>   of His way,
> The first of His works of old.
> I was set up from everlasting, from the beginning,
> Or ever the earth was.
> When there were no depths, I was brought forth ;
> When there were no fountains abounding with water.
> Before the mountains were settled,
> Before the hills was I brought forth ;
> While as yet He had not made the earth, nor the fields,
> Nor the beginning of the dust of the world.

> *   *   *   *

> Now therefore, ye children, hearken unto me ;
> For happy are they that keep my ways.
> Hear instruction, and be wise.
> And refuse it not.

You see, therefore, from this fine passage
that the Torah was in God's possession
before ever He created the world. "Yes, but
why do the Rabbis assume that God made
use of this Torah for the work of creation ?"

you will ask again. The Rabbis have their answer ready, " Look at the first verse of the Torah itself. Does it not say, *Bereshis*, ' In the beginning ' God created the heavens and the earth ? And cannot *Be-reshis* mean that *Be*, בְּ, with (with the help of) *Reshis*, רֵאשִׁית, the Torah (which, as you saw in the above quotation from Proverbs, is called *Reshis*, רֵאשִׁית) God created the heavens and the earth ? " Ingenious, is it not ?

And now comes the main point of this clever, fanciful " play upon words " which the Rabbis loved so much.

It was just because the world was created in accordance with the Torah plan-book, that the work was found to be accurate and sound, good and beautiful : " And the Lord saw all that He had made, and behold it was very good." And this world of ours will continue to be good and beautiful as long as the people in it keep to the plans and designs laid down in the great Book, and remain loyal to the teachings of the Torah.

May I remind you of what a great Jewish teacher once said :—

" Each one of us is a small world in himself," and we must keep on building it up. But for building properly one must have plans. May I therefore commend to you the use of the old, but ever-wonderful and precious book of plans—the Torah—for the building up of this little world of yours, I mean your own selves, your character, your life ? For in that precious book of designs—the Torah, the Law of God—are laid down the principles and rules, according to which we can best regulate our conduct and fashion our lives. How right it is that *Simchas Torah*, the rejoicing in the Law, should come immediately before *Shabbas Bereshis*, the story of creation. Joy in the Law must come before the work of building. And if we build on Torah plans, then will our work pass muster, when it is surveyed by those who are competent to judge, and more especially by God Himself, who is the Chief Inspector, the Great Architect and Master-builder. And the verdict on our labours will certainly be : " Behold everything that we have done is very good."

CHILDREN AS BUILDERS

In the Bible frequent reference is made to children, and the words by which they are described are very pretty and suggestive. They are called " a heritage of the Lord ", " a reward from God ", " a mother's joy ", and " the parents' crown ".

Naturally these beautiful phrases apply chiefly to good children, for troublesome ones, we are told in the same Book, are a source of constant worry and annoyance. " A wise child makes the father glad ", we read in the Book of Proverbs, " but a foolish child is the heaviness of his mother." Again, in the Book of Psalms, in one of the " Songs of Degrees " (which are read at the Sabbath afternoon service during the winter season) children are compared to " olive plants ". For like the olive plants which grow beautiful in good, clear, and soft soil, and yield, under gentle pressure, good oil that produces light and joy, so do children grow good amidst healthy surroundings and yield what is best in them under the gentle discipline of parents and teachers.

Besides these there is another comparison concerning children. It is not found in the Bible at all, although by a play upon words, it is based upon a text in Isaiah. It is taken from the Talmud. It occurs twice in the Prayer Book : once in the Friday evening service before *Kiddush,* and once again in the Sabbath morning service after *En Kelohenu.* It is quoted in the name of Rabbi Chanina, who was not only a father of children but also the headmaster of a big school, and who therefore knew the nature and character, the little ways and peculiarities of the younger generation. What was the comparison that this Rabbi used ? " Thy children (בָּנַיִךְ)," he said, " are thy builders (בֹּנַיִךְ)."

Now, children are, in fact, very fond of building. They take a delight in pulling down and breaking up, and then trying to repair and to rebuild. They can be seen doing it at the seaside, raising castles and fortifications out of the sand and pebbles on the seashore. They can be seen at home, too, constructing objects out of cardboard or blocks of wood. Children are builders by nature. But, by calling the younger children "builders", Rabbi Chanina was not thinking of this kind of building. He was thinking of them as builders in another and a more important sense. In the first place they are builders of themselves. They help their parents and their teachers in the building up and formation of their own character and their own little lives. The building up of our character when we are young is of vital importance, if our character is to endure and remain sound when we grow up to be men and women ; for character-building is like house-building. To build a house firmly and securely so that it may resist rain, storm, and wind, several things are essential. By far the most important is a strong and solid foundation built up of strong and durable material. A shaky foundation will endanger the safety of the whole structure.

Now the child is to the man what the

E

foundation is to a house, and the building up of a child's character means laying the foundation for his future conduct in life. Character-building in a child must therefore be made as firm and as sound as possible. The best and safest materials for the purpose are noble actions. " He who practises good deeds," says a Rabbi, " is like unto a man who sets up a strong foundation of hard stone well cemented, so that the floods cannot move it and the rain cannot affect it."

Children are builders also in another respect. They help to build up or destroy the happiness of their parents' home, the discipline of a class, the tone and reputation of a school. The Bible affords many an instance of the effect of children's conduct on the home.

Who does not remember the sad tale of the sudden death of Eli, the aged priest of Shiloh, and the ruin of his house, brought about by the sinful behaviour of his two sons, Hophni and Phineas ? Or who has not read of the trouble and anguish brought on King David by the rebelliousness and disobedience of his own children Absalom and Adonijah ?

On the other hand, children, by their obedience, their gentleness and kindness, have, like Isaac and Samuel, brought joy to their parents, and happiness to their homes.

Finally, children help to build up or pull down the school they attend. It is related in the Talmud of the great Rabbi Gamaliel, the master of an academy—a kind of advanced school or college—that he would not admit into his school any pupil who was not spotless alike in reputation and character, frank in countenance and straightforward in manner. For that wise teacher felt, as indeed all teachers feel, that one undesirable pupil may oft be a stumbling-block to all his companions, that one bad example may infect and ruin a whole class, just as one single child of strong character and kindly nature may influence for good many of his friends, and help to raise the tone of an entire class.

If we wanted a motto for a school, what is more appropriate than "Thy children are thy builders" ?

And rich is the promise to children who are faithful builders; bountiful is their reward. As our saying continues: "Great shall be the happiness of thy children—thy builders."

A CHANUKAH RIDDLE

I KNOW how fond children are of riddles, and I would like to put before you a Chanukah riddle. It is found in the Talmud and may be translated as follows: "You have my light, and I have your light; if you will keep my light I will keep your light."

This sounds rather difficult, and, although it deals with light, leaves one in the dark. I shall therefore try and explain it to you.

You know what "light" is in the ordinary sense. You see plenty of it about you, both natural and artificial. In the day-time you have the light supplied by the sun, and in the night there is the light provided by the moon, the stars, and also by electricity, gas, or candle.

But "light", like many other words in poetry and song, has also a fanciful meaning. You may remember the saying of the Rabbis that when Moses was born the whole house was filled with "light"; or you may have heard people say that good children generally bring light into the home. Light here means cheerfulness and joy, pleasure and satisfaction.

Again, when on Passover night, in the Seder service, we tell the story of the Exodus from Egypt, and thank God for " having brought us out from darkness into light ", we mean by " light "—freedom and relief. And so, one could go on giving heaps of examples to show how often " light " is used in a poetical sense.

Now in the Bible, " light " often stands for the " Law of God ", the Religion which God gave to Israel. Thus, we read in the Book of Proverbs "The Law is light ". " Light " also stands for " life ", for the soul which God breathed into us. The same Book of Proverbs tells us, " The soul of man is the light of God ". So you see that light in the Bible stands both for " law " and for " life ".

Now, I think, you are beginning to guess the meaning of what I have called a Chanukah riddle. It is really a message which comes to us from God ; and, in order to bring the message home to us in a striking manner, it is put in the form of a riddle.

" You have my ' light '," says God to Israel His people ; that means you have charge of the Law, the Religion, which I gave into your keeping ; and " I have your light ", that is, I am the Guardian of your soul, your life. " If you keep My light "— that is, if you take care of and preserve My Law, " I will keep your light "—I will take care of and preserve your life.

Why do I call this a Chanukah riddle ? Because the saying has the nature and form of a riddle, and applies to the Feast of Chanukah. What is the main point in the story of Chanukah, and why is it kept ? Look up your Prayer Book. You will find the reason given very briefly in the paragraph headed *Al Hannissim* (עַל הַנִּסִּים), which we add in the Amidah during Chanukah.

" It was in the days of the Hasmoneans, Mattathias, the son of Johanan, the High Priest, and his sons, when the wicked power of Greece rose up against Thy people Israel to make them forget Thy Law and to force them to transgress the statutes of Thy will, then didst Thou in Thine abundant mercy rise up for them in the time of their trouble. . . ."

The full story of the struggle and the victory, you should read in the books of the Maccabees, which form part of the collection of books known as the Apocrypha.

Antiochus, the Syrian king, was a very foolish ruler. He did not understand, as for example, the English do, the art of governing a country inhabited by different peoples.

The British Empire embraces many groups such as Jews, Christians, Mahommedans, and others who follow different religions. Each group is allowed to worship God in its own way, according to its beliefs and customs, and the services which these different peoples render to King and Country are not a bit less useful on that account. Just the contrary. Take the Jewish subjects of the British Empire. The more faithful and loyal they are to their religion, the more true are they to the duties of citizenship.

But the foolish Antiochus thought differently. He insisted that all his subjects should be of the same religion. And he therefore forced the Jews to give up their own faith and follow the worship of his heathen gods. If the Jews of that time had given way, what a calamity it would have been, not alone for themselves, but also for the whole world! The Jewish religion would have disappeared, its teachings would have been lost, and the world would have continued to grope in darkness. What was it that put a stop to this great peril? It was the courage of the Maccabees. They roused the people to a sense of duty. They fought like heroes and led the people to victory. They succeeded in cleansing the Temple which the enemy had made unclean with the heathen images put there. They rekindled the light which their foes had put out. The Maccabees saved Judaism from being lost; and, when Judaism was saved, the Jewish people were saved with it. And the world was saved too.

What does the Chanukah riddle say?

"If you keep my light, I shall keep your light." The Maccabees kept God's light—they saved the Law and true Religion ; and God in return kept our "light"—He preserved the "life" of the Jewish people. It is in honour of that great historic event, that we celebrate the Feast of Chanukah and kindle the *lights*.

It is for very good reason that the command to kindle the Chanukah light applies to everyone; to children as well as to grown-ups. In many Jewish houses boys and girls take great pride in trimming and lighting their own special little lamps, for these Chanukah lights stand for Torah and Religion.

If the ancient light of Judaism is to be kept burning in its full brightness, to warm and to cheer us now as it did our forefathers in the past, then all of us must try to keep this light in proper trim ; you, children, no less than we, your elders. You must study the Torah and observe its commands. You must learn to love your religion and feel a pride in it. Like the Maccabees, you must resist with all your strength every attempt, open or concealed, made to entice you away from the faith of your fathers. You must cling to it with all your heart and guard it with all your might.

And if you help us to keep God's light—our Torah, our Religion, our Faith—then you will help towards the fulfilment of God's promise to us in the Chanukah riddle : " If you keep my light, I shall keep your light." Our life and our soul, as well as the life and soul of the Jewish people, will be safe from all hurt. And yours will be the glory, a truly Maccabean glory, of having stood sentinel and been faithful to the great trust.

SEDER SYMBOLS

ALL children are question marks; they ask
questions. The Passover *Haggadah*—the
Seder Service Book—mentions four types
of inquisitive children; the silent, the simple,
the wicked, and the wise. The difference
between the last two is that the wicked child
asks in a sneering sort of way, seeking an
excuse for not doing the things he ought to do;
while the wise one seeks to know the why
and the wherefore of observances, so that he
may carry them out more intelligently.
Questions prompted by the desire to gain
knowledge are most praiseworthy. Did not
Moses, the Lawgiver, in his famous farewell
song, advise: "Ask thy father and he will
tell thee, thy elders and they will explain
to thee"? Likewise, the Jewish sages
have encouraged all honest questionings.
For, they said, "the bashful one does not
learn."

The Seder night is the children's special
" question night ". And no wonder. The
table is decked with many things, strange
and picturesque—quite a museum. The
children's curiosity is aroused to the highest
pitch. And the parents are there, like guides
in that museum, ready to explain. They
regard it as a pleasure to carry out the
Biblical command, " And thou shalt tell
thy child."

All of you, I know, are always prepared
with four set questions. You will guess that
I am referring to the *Mah Nishtannoh*
(מַה נִשְׁתַּנָּה), "Why is this night so
different from other nights ? "

But keen and observant children will not
confine themselves to these regular questions.
They will ask again and again ; and the more
they do, the more we shall be pleased. For,
after all, the Seder table is largely set for
their special benefit.

We do all we can to keep them interested
and to give them a part in the proceedings.
In olden times nuts were shared out to keep
the children awake. Now we let them snatch

and hide away the Afikomon, to keep them amused.

What a large number of unspoken questions must pass through your mind at the Seder table. Let me, therefore, explain the meaning of some of the Seder Symbols.

First there is the Matzo—the unleavened bread, the bread of affliction—a reminder of the hurried deliverance from Egyptian bondage. Let us lift up the cloth that covers it on the table.

You will observe there are three whole Matzos laid in the dish for the Seder ceremony. On Sabbaths and Festivals, as you know, we have only two whole loaves. In Hebrew they are called *Lechem Mishneh*—a double portion. These two loaves are a reminder of the fact that in the wilderness God gave Israel a double portion of manna on Friday to last over the Sabbath. On the Seder night, however, we need three Matzos. The top one we require for the blessing, *Hammotzi* (הַמּוֹצִיא), the usual Grace before meals. The middle one (which we break in two to make it appear all the more as the " bread of affliction ") we need partly for the other blessing, *Al Achilas Matzo* (עַל אֲכִילַת מַצָּה), concerning the eating of unleavened bread, and partly for hiding away as that *Afikomon* upon which your eyes and minds are so keenly fixed. The third Matzo we use for the *Korech* (כּוֹרֵךְ), the portion of Matzo and Morror which we eat together, as the good and peaceful Hillel was wont to do in Temple times.

Next in the Seder-dish is the Morror, the bitter herb, and the Charoses, a preparation made of apples, nuts, cinnamon, and wine. It is rather nice to dip the Morror in Charoses. The latter lessens the actual taste of bitterness; but in reality the sweet Charoses, like the bitter Morror, is a reminder of slavery. For the Charoses is made to resemble the colour of bricks and mortar, and so recalls the labour of brick-making to which our ancestors were forced in the land of Egypt.

Then there is the Shank-bone. It recalls to us the Paschal offering, which is itself a symbol of Israel, for in the books of the Prophets and in the Psalms, Israel is often called the "lamb". And here comes a pretty thought. The lamb as a Paschal offering was to be served up whole. No bone was allowed to be broken. The Jewish people, represented by the lamb, must also remain one united whole and unbroken. And so you will notice that the shank-bone on the Seder-table is not as bare as it appears. It is indeed full of ideas.

Lastly there is the egg. It is introduced in the Seder-dish for several reasons. It recalls the Festival offering which in Temple times was brought in addition to the Paschal lamb. "But why select the egg to remind us of the Festival offering?" you will rightly ask. Well, there is a good reason. In Jewish practice the egg is the special food of people who mourn the loss of someone near and dear to them. Now, on Seder night, amidst all our rejoicing, we do remember with sorrow something we had lost—Jerusalem and the Temple. Again, the egg, from which springs forth new life, is also a sign of hope and expectation, and on Seder night we do think and speak of hope and expectation. We speak

and sing of the restoration of Jerusalem and
the rebuilding of the Temple in such hymns
as the *Addir Hu* (אַדִּיר הוּא) and in the
final prayer, "Next year in Jerusalem"
(לְשָׁנָה הַבָּאָה בִּירוּשָׁלַיִם).

Now as to the wine. On the Jewish
Festivals we have two cups of wine at meal
times : one for Kiddush before the meal,
and the other for Grace after the meal.
On Seder night we have two extra cups,
over which the Hallel and other special
hymns are sung. The four cups of wine on
this night of freedom have been said to
correspond with the four expressions used
in God's promise of Israel's deliverance :
" I shall bring out ", " I shall deliver ", " I
shall redeem ", " I shall take ".

As a matter of fact some Rabbis discovered
five such expressions in the text, the fifth
being : " I shall bring them in." And so, for
this expression, we have a fifth cup. We
name it the Cup of Elijah, in readiness for
the prophet who will come again one day
and decide all doubtful points of Jewish
law. We are therefore not allowed to drink

F

the fifth cup, but let it remain full throughout the Seder, for we await Elijah's coming with eagerness.

Isn't it a pretty idea to introduce Elijah into the Seder celebration ? Some think that the opening of the street-door during the Seder was to give a more real impression of the entry of Elijah into our homes on Passover night.

But the opening of the door now is really a reminder of olden times, the Middle Ages, the days of the Ghetto, when Jews lived under conditions of constant dread among unfriendly peoples who were ready to bring all sorts of cruel and unfounded accusations against them especially at the Passover season. The doors of Jewish houses were repeatedly opened during the Seder Service, and they were opened for two reasons : to see that no danger was lurking without, and to welcome any stray Jews who might be fleeing from trouble, seeking refuge and shelter. To welcome strangers is to welcome Elijah, for he stands for the spirit of Fellowship, Goodwill, and Peace. This spirit hovers over the whole of our Seder celebrations.

On Seder night children and parents meet in a bond of increased affection, recalling together the story of the Jewish people, their sufferings and their hopes, praying, rejoicing, and singing together.

The hearts of parents are turned to their children and the hearts of children unto their parents.

THINGS HOLY AND BEAUTIFUL

On the seventh day of Passover the reading from the Law in Synagogue includes the song sung by the Children of Israel after crossing the Red Sea, and known as the Song of Moses. You will find it, of course, in the Bible—in the Book of Exodus, and also in the Prayer Book as part of the daily service.

In some Synagogues this song is chanted to a special tune, slightly varied from the one used for the reading of the Law on ordinary Sabbaths and Festivals. This special tune is both ancient and pretty. It has been adopted from the Spanish and Portuguese ritual, or service, where the Song of Moses is sung to this tune every Sabbath morning during prayers. And why is this Song of Moses chanted with special joy even in our own Synagogues on the seventh day of Passover ? Because it speaks of the crossing of the Red Sea and the complete deliverance of the Israelites from the pursuing

Egyptians. These happenings took place on the twenty-second day of Nisan, seven days after they had left Egypt which is called the "House of Bondage". "Then sang Moses and the children of Israel this Song." Our ancestors sang it in chorus ; Moses led, and the people took up the refrain. You might re-read the Song, and try to find out which verses you think were sung by Moses, the leader, and which parts were chanted by the Israelites, who, as it were, formed the mighty choir. It would be an interesting exercise. And there is a special reason why you, children, should try your hand at it. The Song is, in a way, also a children's song. When it was first sung on the banks of the Red Sea the children formed part of the great choir of a whole people. " Then sang Moses and the *Children* of Israel " might be taken literally. For, as the Rabbis love to remind us, the young, equally with the old, saw God's wonders at that hour. They joined heartily, as children can, in the hymn of praise for God's mighty deliverance. As you would expect, this Song of Moses resounds with battle cries and shouts of triumph. But, on the other hand, this song is not without its quiet and peaceful notes. It speaks of the entry and settlement of Israel in the Land of Promise : " Thou shalt bring them and plant them in the mountain of Thine inheritance." It speaks of God as the Sovereign Ruler and King : " The Lord shall reign for ever and ever," " And the Lord shall be King over all the earth."

And the Song speaks also of the building of a Sanctuary, or a Temple in which God will dwell and Israel will worship. The Sanctuary, the Rabbis tell us, must be beautiful. " This is my God and I shall glorify Him (וְאַנְוֵהוּ)," says our Song. " Glorify Him, how ? " ask the Rabbis. And this is their reply : " Glorify God, by making the Sanctuary—the Synagogue—as beautiful (נָאֶה) as possible." And not the Sanctuary alone should be beautiful, but also all objects used in the ceremonies of the home, and in the Synagogue Service. We make a handsome Succah, choose a beautiful Esrog, buy a nice Tallis. This rule of the Rabbis has been observed by pious Jews in all lands and at all times. To take a few familiar examples : the front of the Ark is covered with a lovely *Poroches* (פָּרוֹכֶת) or curtain ; an embroidered *Mappoh* (מַפָּה) covers the Reading desk or Almemar ; there are the appointments of the Sepher Torah, the Scroll of the Law ; the binder, the mantle and the cover ; the *Etz Chayyim* (עֵץ חַיִּים) or handles, the *Keser* (כֶּתֶר) or crown, the plate, the bells, the *Yod* (יָד) or pointer— all these have been made of choice material and pretty design.

In our homes we have the Sabbath lamp, the *Kiddush* and *Havdoloh* cup, the *Besomim* (spice) box, the *Seder* dish, the *Esrog* box, the *Chanukah* lamp, the *Megillah* case and many other things. Not that it makes any difference to God in whose service these objects are used. They are marks of *our* reverence and love of God and our respect for His service. We express this love and respect by a longing to worship Him in all the beauty of holiness. I wonder if you recognize the phrase, " to worship God in

the beauty of holiness," and remember
where it comes from ? It is taken from the
twenty-ninth Psalm which is sung in
Synagogue when the Scroll of the Law is
returned to the Ark on Sabbaths after the
Reading is completed. It is a Psalm in the
singing of which you all join. This is how it
begins : " Give unto the Lord, O ye children
of the Mighty, give unto the Lord glory and
strength. Give unto the Lord the glory
due unto His name ; worship the Lord in
the beauty of holiness."

In Palestine to-day, among the public
buildings outside the city of Jerusalem,
there stands, towering up, the Jewish School
of Arts and Crafts. It is called, most
appropriately, the Bezalel School. You will
remember that Bezalel was the clever artist
and craftsman who carried out the building of
the Tabernacle in the wilderness and the
designing of its sacred furniture. In this
Palestinian Jewish Art School are made
many things of art and beauty, including
objects used in the service of the Synagogue
and the ceremonies of the home. You might

have seen some of these objects of Jewish art
in the Palestine Pavilion of the British
Empire Exhibition held some time ago at
Wembley.   There were Chanukah lamps,
Mezuzah cases, Esrog boxes, curtains for
the Ark and mantles for the Scrolls, all
designed with a Jewish touch and worked
after a Jewish pattern in silver, olive-wood,
lace, and silk.   These objects are meant to
lend Jewish colour to the *Hadras Kodesh*,
" the beauty of holiness," in the Synagogue
service and home ceremonies, and so to
glorify God aright.   This   endeavour   to
worship God in a dignified way, to carry out
each Mitzvoh (religious duty) in becoming
and beautiful manner, is called in Hebrew
Hiddur   Mitzvoh (הִדּוּר מִצְוָה).   Our Rabbis
refer to it again and again and highly
commend it, but at the same time they would
have us remember that *the* most important
object of all that we should keep in proper
trim, beautify and prepare with all care
and attention for Divine service in the
Synagogue or home is our own selves—our
hearts, our minds : in the words of the

Song of Moses : " This is my God and *I* shall glorify Him." I—in my person, in my bearing, in my behaviour, in my conduct, in my life.

A JEWISH RIP VAN WINKLE

ONE of the most interesting chapters in the
Bible is the story of the famous friendship
between David and Jonathan. You know the
story well. It is told most charmingly in
the first book of Samuel. David, by his
faithfulness and courage as a shepherd and
warrior, gained the admiration and praise
of Saul's subjects. The King grew jealous
and eyed David with suspicion and distrust.
He was afraid of David. This fear steadily
increased, and turned into bitter hatred.
Saul planned David's death, and made
repeated attempts to carry out his evil
intentions.

But, unlike his father, Jonathan, Saul's
son, was well disposed towards David. Again
and again he tried to plead with his father
on behalf of his blameless friend.

But when his efforts failed, Jonathan
advised David to go away, and arranged
to give a signal of his father's intentions by

shooting arrows in a certain direction. This arrangement assisted David in making good his escape. The friendship between the two became greatly strengthened. They parted from each other with kisses and tears; and Jonathan said, " Go in peace . . . The Lord be between me and thee."

Ancient history, both Roman and Greek, has many a tale to tell of loving souls knit together in close friendship. But none of those instances possesses the charm and fine touches which distinguish this friendship of David and Jonathan.

You will remember the words of David in his famous lamentation over Saul and Jonathan, his son, in which he speaks of Jonathan in the following terms : " I am distressed for thee, my brother Jonathan; very pleasant hast thou been unto me ; wonderful was thy love to me."

Friendship of this kind is very rare. But there are friendships which everyone can make, and which everyone ought to make. For, says Ben Sira, a wise man who lived in Palestine two thousand years ago, " A faithful

friend is like medicine." He acts like a tonic ;
he makes us strong.

There is a pretty story told in the Talmud,
something like the story of Rip Van Winkle
of which you may have heard. It is about
a teacher and miracle-worker who lived in
the first century. His name was Choni
Hameaggel, which means " Onias the circle-
drawer ". The origin of the name is rather
interesting. It is related that there was
once a drought, a very dry period, in
Palestine which lasted a whole month. In
Palestine, which depended for its water
entirely on the rain, the lack of it was a
terrible calamity. The people had prayed
for rain but without result. They came
to Choni or Onias, since he was known to be
a very pious man, and asked him to pray
to God for them. Choni thereupon drew a
circle on the ground with his staff. He
placed himself in the centre of it, began to
pray, and, full of confidence, said that he
would not move from the spot until his
prayer was answered. His prayer was
answered, and rain came down. After this,

Choni, the circle-drawer, fell asleep for seventy years. When he awoke, he found the world around him completely changed, the old familiar faces gone, and himself left without comrades. He felt so lonely and depressed, that he prayed, " Give me friendship or give me death." God heard his prayer, and he died.

Choni's cry is not difficult to understand. For the joys of life cannot be really enjoyed without a true friend to whom we can speak about them, or who can share them with us. On the other hand, troubles and worries lose half their sting with a faithful friend or companion to help to bear them. And friendship does even more. It acts as a healthy influence upon life and conduct. It helps to keep us straight and honest. For a true friend is one with whom we exchange confidences, to whom we entrust many of our secrets. And once we feel we must reveal our thoughts and our actions to a friend, we naturally take care that the thoughts and actions should be such that we are not ashamed to own them. In this way

a friend acts as a kind of check upon our
conduct in life. We are sure to be less
conceited, less selfish, less revengeful, if we
have the good and true friend to curb and
control us.

The Rabbis, therefore, again and again
urge us to get a companion or friend.
" Provide thyself a teacher and get thee a
companion," says one of the sages in the
Pirke Aboth or " Ethics of the Fathers ".
" Which is the good way to which a man
should cling ? " a famous Rabbi (Rabbi
Jochanan ben Zakkai) once asked of his
disciples. And one of them rightly replied,
" A good friend, a good companion." For
a good friend, a good companion, helps one
to go the right way. Companionship further
prevents us from becoming stale and dull ;
it helps us to grow in knowledge. As the
wise king says in the Book of Proverbs :
" Even as iron sharpeneth iron, so do companions sharpen one another." But our
Rabbis insist upon the choice of the right
kind of companion and friend. In the same
chapters of the Ethics of the Fathers, where

we are advised to get us a companion, we are warned : "Associate not with the wicked." It must be a good companion, a good friend, that we are to seek and to choose. For a bad friend, a bad companion is ever so much worse than none at all. The Rabbis themselves prayed, " O lead us not into the power of sin or of transgression, or of iniquity or of temptation . . . *keep us far from a bad man, and a bad companion ;*" and this prayer they bade us repeat daily, ere we started forth to meet our fellow-men. " Every bird associates with one of its kind, and every man with his like," says Ben Sira, the wise man elsewhere referred to. It is the same as the modern proverb : " Birds of a feather flock together." By associating with a bad companion, we ourselves are likely to be branded as bad. And what is worse still, we may actually become as bad as our bad companions. For he who keeps company with the evil-minded and impure, is in danger of becoming so himself. A bad companion leads one to temptation and sin. And so, whilst trying to get companions and make friends, be sure that they are of the right kind.   And if you are careful in your choice, you may have the good fortune of striking up a friendship which will be as sweet, and as genuine, and as lasting as the friendship of David and Jonathan.

CHILDREN AS PLEDGES

IF you were asked for a list of Feasts and Festivals which have a special interest for children, I doubt if you would think of including the Festival of Shovuos in the same way as you would the Festival of Passover, with its children's Seder ceremony, or the Feast of Chanukah with its children's services.

And yet, in olden times, Shovuos, or the Feast of Weeks, was very much of a children's festival, and had a great number of attractions for the younger members of the congregation.

For, with this Festival of the Jewish Year was associated a very attractive children's ceremony. It resembled somewhat the Barmitzvah celebration of the present day, but was even more interesting and more joyous in its nature.

Shovuos was the Festival on which young children, chiefly boys, were introduced for the first time to the Hebrew School. Some of you may smile. There is nothing very fascinating, you will tell me, about going to school ; certainly nothing very enticing or jolly about beginning new lessons.

But let me describe what exactly took place. Early on Shovuos morning, the young boy, who was as much a hero then as the Barmitzvah lad is now, was dressed in a new suit well provided with pockets. This fact at once filled the child with joyful hopes. And he was not disappointed. For, as soon as he was ready to leave home, these pockets were generously filled with different kinds of fruit, and with sweet cakes on which were stamped in Hebrew letters simple texts in praise of the Torah, the Jewish Law, and its study.

Thus richly laden with dainties, the happy child was taken to the flower-decked Synagogue ; for on Shovuos the Synagogues were decorated with flowers and plants then as they are to-day. He was placed on the Almemar in the centre of the Synagogue, and permitted to listen to the reading from the Law.

When this was finished, the child was

conducted to the schoolroom. There he received his first lesson in Hebrew by eating up those sweet cakes with the honeyed letters marked upon them. How the child must have enjoyed this first lesson! He probably wished that it had lasted much longer. It certainly made him anxious to revisit the Hebrew school. But why was Shovuos selected for this very interesting ceremony of introducing the Jewish child to Talmud Torah, the study of the Jewish Law, and of thus dedicating him to the service of God?

The reason is obvious. Because Shovuos is the Festival of the Law. True, Shovuos is also "the Feast of the Harvest"—*Chag Hakkotzir* (חַג הַקָּצִיר), and "the Day of the First Ripe Fruits" — *Yom Habbikkurim* (יוֹם הַבִּכּוּרִים). On this festival, which marks the end of seven weeks after the first day of Passover, an offering from the first ripe fruits of the land was brought to the Temple. But Shovuos is more especially the Festival of the Law, kept to celebrate the giving of the Ten Commandments on

Mount Sinai in the third month, the month of Sivan, in the second year after the children of Israel had come out of Egypt. In the Prayer Book, this Festival is called *Zeman Mattan Torosenu* (זְמַן מַתַּן תּוֹרָתֵנוּ), the Season of the giving of our Law. And can you imagine a more suitable occasion for a child to begin to learn the Law than Shovuos, the Festival of the Law ?

There is a very pretty story, told in the name of Rabbi Meir, which brings out even more clearly the connection between the children's ceremony I have described and the Feast of Weeks.

When the Israelites had gathered at the foot of Mount Sinai, ready and willing to receive the promised Law, God said to them, " I am about to present you with the most precious of treasures, a gift beyond compare. The possession of this gift will bring not only satisfaction and joy to yourselves but peace and happiness to the whole world. For ' its ways are ways of pleasantness, and all its paths are peace '. What pledge, what guarantee, what security will you offer that this treasure, this gift of the Law, will be properly guarded and safely preserved throughout the generations ? " " Think of our pious ancestors, Abraham, Isaac, and Jacob," Israel replied. " Is not our glorious past a sufficient guarantee that the Law will be safe in our hands ? " " No," came God's answer, " such a guarantee is not good enough. I cannot accept it. For no people can exist on its past alone. No nation can live solely by the merits of its Fathers."

" Then, think of the Prophets who will arise in our midst ; of the great men in every generation who will uphold the Law in days to come. Let them be the guarantee," pleaded the Israelites. " No," again came the answer, " This pledge also I cannot accept. For a people's treasures cannot properly be preserved and made to become the possession of all by the reverence and loyalty of a number of chosen ones alone."

At last the Israelites after much thought offered their children as security. " Our children," they exclaimed, " shall be our

pledges.   For we shall ever try to introduce
all our boys and girls to the study of the
Law, and train them in the practice of
Religion."

" Truly an excellent security ! " came
God's reply, " This pledge I accept." And
Israel became the proud possessor of the
Law of Life.

This pretty story, adds R. Meir, is recalled
by the words of the Psalmist who says :
" Out of the mouth of babes and sucklings
hast Thou founded strength." For it was
through the pledge of our children and the
promise of their studying the Law, that
the Torah—the tower of strength—was given
to Israel.

To show how well they remembered the
solemn promise, given by our ancestors at
the foot of Sinai, the Jews in olden days
made it a practice to introduce their children
for the first time to the Synagogue and School
on Shovuos, the anniversary of the giving
of the Law.

And when Jewish children, girls and boys,
show themselves keen upon the study of the

Law, and try loyally to keep its teaching, they help us to redeem the old pledge and fulfil the old promise given by our forefathers at Sinai when they exclaimed : " Our children shall be our pledges."

THE LANGUAGE OF FLOWERS

HAVE you ever heard of the language known as the language of flowers and plants? In this language, which belongs to no special country or people but is understood everywhere, different flowers and plants express different ideas.

Thus, for example, the red rose means beauty, brightness, and love. The perfumed violet stands for trust and modesty, while the pearly daisy and the white lily have always been taken as pictures of innocence and purity. In this language, the olive or olive-branch speaks of peace; the laurel stands for glory; the anemone suggests hope; the never-fading amaranth points to immortality, or life after death. This poetic meaning of nature was carefully observed and largely used by the writers of the Hebrew Bible; whilst the Rabbis of the Talmud, in explaining sacred Scripture, lent additional charm and beauty to the touches of nature in the Biblical text.

If you read the Bible carefully, you will
not fail to notice how familiar the Prophets
and the Psalmists were with the sound and
meaning of the world of nature.

The green grass, the fair flowers, the tall
trees, spoke to them in clear accents and
plain language. They spoke of God and man,
of Israel and the nations, of life in the present
and in the world to come.

You will find many such examples in all
the books of the Bible, but especially in the
Song of Songs and in the Psalms. Let me
give you an instance from one of these
Psalms contained in the Prayer Book. You
remember the well-known Psalm, which is
headed, " A Psalm of Song for the Sabbath
Day ". There we read, " The righteous
shall blossom like a palm-tree, like a cedar
in Lebanon he shall grow ". Just think a
moment, and you will realize how apt and
beautiful is the comparison. The stately
cedar of Lebanon, towering up lofty and
strong ; the beautiful palm-tree, growing
luxuriant in barren and dry soil, drawing
its sap from a secret source—what fine

figures they are for the truly righteous man who remains faithful and loyal in spite of his surroundings, strong in his convictions, firm in his faith !

Again, in the same Psalm we read, " The wicked spring up as grass, the workers of iniquity flourish ". Yes, they spring up and flourish, but only like the grass and flowers, quickly to fade away and disappear for ever. I shall leave you to search out other examples for yourselves.

But on this Festival of Shovuos, the Festival of the Law, you might like to hear something about the way in which the poets of the Bible and the sages of the Talmud spoke of the Torah through the language of nature. The Torah has been pictured under the figure of water. Like water, it comes from on high ; it purifies and refreshes. The Torah also for the strength and sweetness, the cheerfulness and comfort it brings, is likened unto wine and oil, honey and milk. Hence the custom to eat milk food on Shovuos, the Festival of the Law. " And ", adds a Jewish Rabbi, "even as these liquids are very rarely stored in vessels of silver and gold, but are best preserved in plain vessels of earthenware, so are Torah and Religion best preserved in those people who are simple in their habits and modest in their ways."

And this reminds me of a story. Rabbi Joshua ben Chananiah, one of the wittiest and most learned Rabbis of his age, was not blessed with personal beauty. One day the daughter of Hadrian, the Roman Emperor, said to him in a mocking manner : " Imagine such excellent knowledge in so plain a container ! " " But," retorted the sage, " does not your royal father store his best wines in plain earthenware vessels ? " " In what else, pray, should he store them ? " she said. " Surely," replied the Rabbi, " a person in such high position should store his wines in vessels of silver and gold." She pressed the suggestion upon her father, who, to please his daughter, transferred the wine into vessels of silver and gold. The wine turned sour. When the report reached the Emperor he inquired who it was that had given the wrong   advice.   " Rabbi   Joshua   ben

Chananiah," replied the daughter. The Rabbi was summoned into the royal presence and was asked the reason for such a foolish suggestion. " To cure your daughter of her mocking ways," answered the Rabbi. " For now she will realize that even as the choicest wines are stored in the plainest of vessels, so are knowledge and piety best preserved in persons who are free from outward vanity and show."

But the Torah is compared with yet another object of nature. The Law is called a Tree of Life. " It is a tree of life to those who uphold it," we sing in chorus as the Scroll of the Law is put back into the Ark. This likeness of the Law—or the Jewish Religion—to a tree, is very striking. A living tree, as you know, has roots and branches, blossoms and fruit. Likewise the Torah has roots and branches, namely, its principles and off-shoots. Like the tree, the Torah also has its blossoms and fruit—its customs and its ceremonies.

In a tree the roots and the branches, the blossoms and the fruit, are closely connected with one another. And one can generally judge the healthiness of the roots and the soundness of the branches by the fairness of the flowers, the beauty of the blossoms, and the goodness of the fruit. Even so, one can tell the strength of a person's religion, the soundness of his principles, his convictions, and his faith by the outward signs of his religious life, by the nobility of his conduct and the righteousness of his actions.

As the roots of a tree are set deep in the soil, so must the roots of religion be set deep down in the heart. The fruits must be visible to the outside world—in life, in action, and in conduct.

Year after year, on the Festival of Shovuos, the Day of the First Ripe Fruits, we introduce into our Synagogues some of Nature's gifts. We decorate the House of Worship with fair plants and sweet-smelling flowers, and we feast our eyes upon their charm and beauty. We listen to their language, as they speak to us of God's gracious goodness in making the world so full of beauty and rich in bounties. But Shovuos is also the Festival of the Law. And so these flowers that fade and these plants that wither must direct our hearts and minds to that heavenly plant, the Torah, which remains for ever fresh and sweet. " Grass withereth and flowers fade, but the word of our God endureth for ever," is the Psalmist's song.

Now the Law is not only a living tree, it is also a life-giving tree. " The Law is a tree of life." Upon it depends our very life and existence. " Like the days of the tree are the days of my people," exclaims the prophet Isaiah. Israel will last as long as the tree of the Torah lasts. Whilst Judaism lives, we, the Jewish people, live also ; and with its strength, we too gain strength.

JEREMIAH

" THE Three Weeks "—this is the name given to the period of the year between the Fast of the seventeenth of Tammuz and *Tisho be - Ov* (תִּשְׁעָה בְּאָב), the Fast of the ninth day of Av.

It is one of the saddest periods in the history of our people. It brings back the sorrowful events which led up to the destruction of Israel's two Temples.

It was during this period that the First Temple, built more than two thousand years ago with so much grandeur by King Solomon, was reduced to ruins by Nebuchadnezzar, King of Babylon.

It was also during this period of the year, but very much later, that the Second Temple, of still greater glory, built in the days of Ezra and Nehemiah, was burned down to ashes by Titus, the Roman general.

At the sad time of the destruction of the First Temple there lived a very great man.

His name was Jeremiah. We read about him in the Haphtorah on the first Sabbath in the "Three Weeks". You can learn a great deal about a man by reading the books he has written, because a man's work is often the key to his character. Would you like to read about Jeremiah ? An account can be found in the Bible, in the book called "Jeremiah". The book of Jeremiah is almost an autobiography, which means the life-story of a person written by himself. It is intensely interesting as it contains a good deal of history and it is not difficult even for children to read and understand.

From this book we get a picture of the man and a glimpse into his character and his qualities. And what a remarkable personality you will find him to be !

There is one special quality which shines out with particular brilliance in the life of Jeremiah. It is his deep devotion to duty ; his firmness in fulfilling it at all times. The call of duty—to go and speak in God's name—came to him very early in life. At first

H

Jeremiah would not accept the task. " I
am still young," he pleaded, " too young to
undertake such work." Children and young
people often make the same plea when something to do comes their way. " Oh, plenty
of time yet," you will hear them say. But
God replied, " Say not ' I am too young'."
One must begin early in life, and by degrees
get into the work, whether it be at school
or in later life. For if one waits too long
before commencing, the opportunity of doing
anything at all may often slip away. Jeremiah
saw the force of these words. He undertook
the task, and having once undertaken it he
persevered with it. He would never shirk
a duty because it was unpleasant. He would
never leave a thing undone just because the
doing of it was rather difficult.

Jeremiah, as I have already told you,
lived during the period of the destruction
of the First Temple. At that time the
people were not " all angels ", as we say.
They are not so now, either ! We know from
the Bible and other Jewish writings that the
destruction of Jerusalem and the Temple

was due largely to the sinfulness of the people.

At such a time it was the painful duty of the true prophet to say things that were unpleasant ; to tell the people things which were perfectly true, but which they did not like to hear ; for people do not always like to hear the truth, especially when the truth is not very complimentary to them. He had to preach peace when the people, the priests, and the false prophets, were all in favour of war. He had to tell them that instead of fighting against Babylon, they should fight against their own evil ways ; to tell them, for example, that their visits to the Temple were useless, even sinful, if the object of these visits was not the real one of prayer and praise, but merely to engage in idle and frivolous talk, in planning mischief and offending God.

Many a man would have shrunk from such a task ; not so Jeremiah. He was true to his duty. He feared and flattered no one. He did not study his own comfort or convenience. " The words," as he himself tells us in his book, " were like a burning fire in his heart." The truth would out, whatever the consequences might be.

Once, so runs the story in his book, Jeremiah went into the potter's yard and there he bought an earthenware bottle. Holding it up in his hand, he marched through the city. The elders in Israel, and the elders among the priests who had led the people astray, were curious to know the meaning of this strange action of the prophet, and followed him in large numbers. Accompanied by these crowds, Jeremiah wended his way to one of the valleys outside Jerusalem. There, in the sight of the men who went out with him, he broke the bottle in pieces. The people looked on with amazement. What did all this mean ? Suddenly Jeremiah exclaimed, " Even so will God break this people and this city, as one breaketh a potter's vessel that cannot be made whole again ! " He then marched back into the city ; he took his stand in the court of the Temple and proclaimed before all the people, " Thus saith the God of Israel, I will bring upon this city and upon all her towns, all the evil that I have spoken against her, because they stiffened their neck so as not to obey my words." In such bold and outspoken manner he repeatedly rebuked the people for their wrong-doing, and urged them to mend their ways.

But if Jeremiah was a man of strong character and iron will, he was at the same time of a gentle and kindly nature with a warm heart full of sympathy.

True to duty, and hoping to get the people to repent and return while there was yet time, Jeremiah warned them of the coming destruction of the Temple and the fate of Israel. On the other hand, when the Temple fell, and the people were led away into exile, he bewailed their misfortune, broke forth into lamentations, and shed bitter tears. These lamentations, called, in Hebrew, *Kinos*, are preserved in the Bible in the Book of Lamentations (אֵיכָה).

When the Temple fell, and Israel went into exile, the king of Babylon offered the prophet safety and comfort; but Jeremiah, who was unselfish and thought only of his people, refused. He preferred to suffer with his people and to share their sorrows. His desire was to be with them, to soothe them, to comfort them, to fill their hearts with hopes of better days to come. His was a fine character ! He combined strength of will, boldness of action, devotion to duty with a wealth of sympathy, a kindliness of nature, and a fullness of love.

Jeremiah, whose name is recalled during " the three weeks ", is one of the great Bible heroes whose writings should be read, whose lives should be studied, and whose examples should be imitated.

Duty's call comes to us all as it did to Jeremiah the Prophet. It comes very early in life. To this call we must respond. Say not, " I am too young." For it is never too early to begin. And the younger one begins to learn the lesson, the more lasting it is likely to be, and the more effective in its results.

IN TOUCH WITH NATURE

" WHO is yonder man that walketh in the field to meet us ? " Now Isaac had gone out " to meditate in the field at eventide."

This is how Isaac, the son of Abraham, is brought into our view, in one of the most interesting Bible stories in the Book of Genesis. Pretty in itself, the tale is made even more charming by many beautiful touches of nature. Let me recall some of the points in the story.

First we have the journey of Eliezer, Abraham's tried and faithful servant, accompanied by a caravan of camels, decked out with the most elaborate trappings, and richly laden with the wealth of their master. Next follows the animated scene at the well, outside the city of Nahor in Mesopotamia, where we can almost hear the shouts of the shepherds, the bleating of the flocks and herds, and the rush of the maidens with pitchers on their shoulders going forth to draw water. Then comes the dramatic appearance of Rebekah, one of the sweetest and most charming of Bible heroines, a model of courtesy and kindness, full of natural grace and affection, busying herself with household work, yet retaining a perfect dignity. And finally there is the homely atmosphere and the festive gathering at the house of Rebekah's parents.

It is in the midst of this group of picturesque scenes that we catch a glimpse of the hero of our story. " And Isaac went out to meditate in the field at eventide." We see him in the darkening evening twilight, roaming alone among the springing grass, the golden grain, and the sweet-smelling flowers, deeply wrapped in silent meditation. You might think perhaps that Isaac was on his country holiday then. No ! These rambles in the country formed part of his regular daily occupation. Isaac, it appears, was a genuine country lad, a true child of nature from his earliest youth. He was born, so tradition tells us, at noon, in the month of Nisan (also called *Oviv,* the spring month), when

the spring sun was shining in all its glory ;
so that nature smiled on him at his very
birth.

It is likewise related that throughout the
days of his youth he showed a strong liking
for the green fields, the open air, and the
healthy outdoor life. This love of nature
which was almost inborn in him grew stronger
as the boy grew older. And one could see
him very often at the decline of day, walking
out among the fields with his eyes open and
all his senses wide awake, pondering deeply
upon the beauties of God's world.

These daily rambles into the country,
this close observation and love of nature,
no doubt had a very marked influence upon
Isaac's character. This constant touch with
things bright and beautiful, wise and wonderful, must have helped to bring out in our
young hero those fine feelings and noble
qualities which he displayed in such marked
degree throughout his life. For Isaac, as
we know, did possess very many excellent
qualities.

In the first place, he was extremely obedient.

You remember the occasion when he was ready
to give up the most precious possession—his
very life—because his father wished it and
God at first willed it so. Again, Isaac was
most generous and most kind, very patient
and very peaceful. You recollect the time
when he gave way to his envious and quarrel-
some neighbours, the Philistines, in the
incident of the wells, rather than create
a scene and quarrel. Isaac was likewise a
model of perseverance, an example of
steadiness and industry.

All this is known from the pages of
Scripture History. Now where did he acquire
these good traits ? In his parents' home,
it will be answered. He learnt them, by
example, from Abraham his father. Quite so.
But, like Abraham his father, Isaac also was
certainly encouraged to develop these
qualities by being brought into close touch
with the world of nature ; by using to the
full his many opportunities, to contemplate
and drink-in the wonders and beauties
of God's creation. As the Bible puts it :
" And Isaac went out to meditate in the

field at eventide." For nature—the handiwork of God—is a fascinating book, rich in the most valuable object lessons, beautifully illustrated and popularly presented.

A Jewish Rabbi once said : " Even if the Law had not been given to Israel, man could have learned many a virtue from the habits of animals and the ways of birds " ; and we might add, also from nature and the growth of plants. This is perfectly correct and very beautifully expressed. Let me illustrate its truth by one or two examples.

Think of the heavens above. Can one imagine a more striking object lesson in cheerful obedience, in regularity and punctuality, than is presented by the sun, the moon, and the countless hosts of stars, which, in the words of our Sabbath prayers, " rejoice in their going forth and are glad in their return, performing with awe the will of their Master " ?

Or turn to nature on the earth beneath. What a wonderful object lesson in faithfulness and gratitude is supplied by the flocks and herds who answer lovingly to their shepherd's call, and hasten at eventide to greet their kindly master. Or what a splendid example in industry and perseverance, in helpfulness and mutual friendliness, is presented by the large swarms of buzzing bees rushing to and fro, gathering sweetness from many a fragrant flower, and turning it into honey which man may enjoy.

Is it necessary to heap up instances ? One might say, in the words of Job to his friend : " Ask now the beasts and they shall teach you, and the fowls of the air and they shall tell you ; or speak to the earth and it shall teach you, and the fowls of the sea shall declare unto you."

Unfortunately, to children living in big crowded cities, the opportunities of getting a glimpse of the country and the true wonders of nature are very few and far between. Our towns have not yet been turned into garden cities. We have many lanes, it is true, but not much sunshine and very little of country air in them.

In London, for example, such places as

Goodman's Fields, Great Garden Street, and Greenfield Street have hardly a blade of grass, a fresh flower, or a shady tree about them to suggest the green fields or the flourishing garden indicated by their names.

You children, I feel sure, must welcome the rare occasions on which you are brought into closer touch with nature.

You must feel very thankful for the annual outings, the country holidays, when you are enabled, like Isaac of old, to go out into real fields, to breathe the fresh air, to bask in the clear sunshine, to gaze upon and enjoy the beauty and loveliness of God's world.

But even throughout the year you must endeavour not to lose touch altogether with nature and country life.

There are public gardens, museums, and schools where you can observe and study nature. There are also your own windows which with very little trouble you can try and turn into so many window gardens; and there is many a plot which, under your gentle care, may be made to grow tender plants, and blush forth into beautiful blossoms and pretty flowers.

This continued touch with nature, this study of the world of wonders will enable you to understand more intelligently the beauties of the country when the next holiday comes round.

And this intelligent grasp of God's world will help you to become better and nobler in your own natures. For like Isaac of old, who *meditated* when roaming alone in the fields, your eyes, minds, and hearts also will turn in deep understanding and fervent love from nature even unto nature's God.

WILLING HANDS AND WILLING HEARTS

EGYPT, where the children of Israel were once slaves, is full of historic interest. It boasts of many famous sights and places of great antiquity. One of these places, not far from the city of Cairo, is particularly interesting. About an hour's drive from the city there is a large plain covered knee-deep with sand. Crowds of people, hailing from different lands, and speaking a variety of languages, assemble there every day. One meets black Arabs on their camels and mules, as well as richly-dressed white men on horseback or in carriages. The confusion of tongues reminds one of the Tower of Babel. And what is the reason for these large gatherings ? They have all come to see one of the most ancient monuments of the world, one of the greatest of its wonders—The Egyptian Pyramids. These Pyramids are gigantic monuments built of glittering granite.

It takes a considerable time to go round them, and, as for height, their tops seem to reach the sky. To gain the summit is, as may well be imagined, not an easy task. Three experienced guides are needed to help you up in safety and prevent you from falling. Once the top is reached, your effort is rewarded by a wonderful view of the land for miles around. These Pyramids were built by Egyptian slaves, and many must have been injured or even killed in building them. And what was the purpose of these gigantic structures, it might be asked ? They are a kind of Temple, raised in honour of some proud and powerful kings. Beneath them lie buried the Pharaohs and the great ones of the land of Egypt. These Pyramids have stood for thousands of years. Our ancestors saw them when they came out of Egypt.

Now, when the Children of Israel passed through the wilderness on their way from Egypt to Canaan, they also built a monument, in honour of their King, the living King, the King of kings—to the glory of God. They built a *Mishkan*, a Tabernacle. But what a contrast was this monument to the huge Egyptian Pyramids, the large heathen Temples.

The Mishkan which the children of Israel built in the wilderness, and about which we read in the Book of Exodus, was neither large nor strong. It was not built with blocks of stone, or even with bricks, like our Synagogues of to-day. It was a plain, simple tent, joined together by narrow boards, and covered with home-spun curtains. It was not firmly set or fixed, but, like a soldier's tent, could be taken to pieces and moved from place to place. You might imagine, perhaps, that God did not think much of this small structure which His children had made for Him. Just the contrary, He was very pleased with it. He liked it as well as if it had been a mighty and magnificent building like the Pyramids which the Egyptians had made. One of the Rabbis of the Midrash who always looked into the deeper meaning, the spirit, behind the words of the Bible, tells us that the Mishkan, the Tabernacle erected in the wilderness, was as dear to

God as if it had been made of fine gold.
God liked the Tabernacle even better than
the Temple which King Solomon afterwards
built in Jerusalem, although this Temple
was much grander and ever so much finer ;
richer in design, and more beautifully
decorated.

Why, do you think, did God like the
Mishkan—the small tent in the wilderness—
so much ? It was because of the right spirit
in which the task of constructing it had been
undertaken, the ready and willing manner
in which it had been carried out. There was
nothing forced about it, nothing unpleasant ;
no need to place taskmasters over the work-
men with whip in hand, as the Egyptians
had done in the building of their cities
and temples ; no necessity even to set
ordinary watchmen to make sure that the
work was done. No sooner was God's desire
expressed, " Let them make Me a Sanctuary,"
than people set about fulfilling God's desire
with all their energy. They put their whole
heart and mind to the task. They did it
with free and willing hands. It was this

spirit of ready willingness which pleased
God so much. It was not exactly *What they
did*, but *How they did it*. For God loves us
to put our whole heart into the work which
we are set to do.

This lesson is repeated again and again
in Jewish teaching. In the *Shema*, for
example, when commanded to love God,
we are told to do so " With all our heart, and
with all our soul, and with all our might ".

We must never do things half-heartedly
or in a slip-shod manner. Whatever the work
we have to do, be it at school, in Synagogue,
at home, or in business, if we do it at all
we should try to do it with all our heart,
and with all our might. As Koheleth, the
great preacher of Wisdom, has well said :
" Whatsoever thy hand attaineth to do, do
it with all thy might " ; and, what is more,
do it pleasantly, and willingly. Then will
your efforts be of the greatest value, and of
the highest good. They will be appreciated
by those to whom they are rendered, and
sooner or later will receive their full reward.

WHAT'S IN A NAME?

"WHAT'S in a name?" asks the poet. Well, there is often much in it. The names of countries, towns or streets often recall facts and fancies in connection with their origin; the names of persons remind us of certain happenings in the life of the parents, the family, or the people to which they belong.

Here are some examples from the Bible :

Noah or *Noach* was so called because, as his father put it, "This child shall comfort us in our work and in the toil of our hands"; (*Noach* נֹחַ was connected with the Hebrew *Nachem* נַחֵם, which means "to comfort").

The third Patriarch was named Jacob יַעֲקֹב, which means in Hebrew "following on the heel" (from *Ekev* עָקֵב, a heel) or coming after someone else. Jacob was called so, because he was the second son of Isaac and Rebekah, born *after* Esau, his elder brother.

116

Some names probably refer to some special qualities of the persons bearing them ; for example, we are told in the Purim Megillah, Esther was called also " Hadassah ", which means Myrtle. It was a kind of pet name and suggested her amiability of nature, and sweetness of temper.

Again, many personal names in the Bible referred to events and hopes not in the lives of individuals, but in the life of the nation as a whole.

The Prophet Isaiah, who foretold the destruction of the Temple and the exile of the people, called one of his sons "Sheor-Yoshuv", meaning " A remnant shall return ". By this name he expressed the hope and prayer that Israel would return to the land of their fathers, from which for a time they would be exiled.

As to Biblical names of places, nearly all of them are connected with events which are recorded in the Bible itself. *Bethel* means " the house of God " and reminds us of the well-known incident in the life of Jacob : the dream, the vow, and the promise. *Achor,*

which means " troubling ", is the name of
a valley and recalls, as with a flash, the story
of Achan's disobedience and the trouble it
brought upon all the people.

There are ever so many other instances ; and
when you read the Bible, you will do well
to look out for them. You will find the
search both fascinating and useful. The
names will help you to fix Biblical events
all the more easily in your minds. Here is
something of more recent interest. At the
end of last century, Jewish "Lovers of Zion"
flocked in large numbers to the Holy Land
to found new colonies, and by labour and toil
to make the waste land of Palestine yield
rich and goodly fruit as in the days of old.
Now, listen to the names which they gave
to the newly-founded colonies : *Rishon
le-Zion*, " The First for Zion," was one ;
Rosh Pinnah, " the Head (or Corner) Stone,"
was another ; *Pethach Tikvah*, " the Door
of Hope," was a third.

But I should like to direct your special
attention to three names by which persons of the Jewish race and faith are

described :   " Hebrews,"   " Jews,"   and
" Israelites".

" Hebrews " (*Ivrim* עִבְרִים) is no doubt
one of the oldest names by which our people
have been known. You remember the story
in the Book of Jonah. It is read as a
Haphtorah on the Day of Atonement. When
Jonah was asked by his fellow-passengers,
what was his name, whence he came, and
what was his occupation, he replied *Ivri
Onochi,* " I am a Hebrew." *Ivrim Anachnu*
" Hebrews are we " is the refrain of a modern
Hebrew song chanted by children in some
Hebrew schools. Again, " Hebrew " עִבְרִית,
as you know, is the name given to the language
in which the Bible and other Jewish books
are written, and which is now spoken by
thousands and thousands of Jews both in
Palestine and outside the Holy Land.

Now, why are we called " Hebrews " ?
Because we are the descendants of Abraham
who was called " Abraham the Hebrew ".
" Hebrews " is therefore a name of distinc-
tion. It shows our old descent, our connection
with the first of the Patriarchs.

Our Rabbis add another pretty explanation of the name. Abraham, they say, was called the " Hebrew " because the word " Hebrew " עִבְרִי means "the person who stands on one side " עֵבֶר. For Abraham was content to stand alone on one side, on the side of God, whilst all the world were gathered against him on the other side, on the side of idol worship. He had the courage of his opinions, and remained firm in his beliefs. And the Jewish people also have remained " Hebrews " in the same sense. They, too, have often stood alone on one side, against a whole world which was opposed to them. They have stood up for justice and truth, for God and goodness.

The second and more familiar name by which we are known is "Jews". The word "Jews" is a kind of short form for "Judeans". This name therefore connects us with Palestine, the " land of Judea ". You will recollect that the Jewish regiment, which in the last Great War went out to help to free Palestine and restore it to its ancient glories, was named " The Judeans ".

And lastly we are called " Israelites ",
or the " Children of Israel ". Israel was
another name given to Jacob, the third
Patriarch, after his weary wanderings and
his great struggle. You remember the story
in the Book of Genesis, which ends : " Thy
name shall be called no more Jacob, but
Israel, for thou hast striven with God and
with men, and hast prevailed."

And we are called " Israelites " or " the
Children of Israel ", because we are the
descendants and followers of Jacob or Israel,
and the Rabbis add a pretty thought on
this last name that we bear. They have put
it in the form of a parable. A king had a
precious jewel box, and a small key which
opened it. " If I leave this small key as it is,"
said he, " it might easily be lost. I shall
therefore attach a chain to it, so that should
the key be mislaid the trailing chain will
help to trace it."

" Even so," said God, " my scattered
people are the key to the world's treasures.
If I leave My people to themselves, they may
be lost among the nations. I shall therefore

fasten My name *El* to them (*El*, אֵל, God, being the last syllable of Isra-el, יִשְׂרָאֵל). This will help to keep them safe; it will guard them against being swallowed up or lost among the peoples. It will enable them to find themselves."

Isn't it a pretty parable?

The chain, which God fastened to the whole of Israel, is linked on to every individual child of Israel. We are all, as it were, attached to Him. As children of Israel, we have the Almighty ever walking with us to help and protect us, and likewise to guide and direct us.

We cannot go astray, or do wrong when we know and feel that *El*, God, is ever by our side. On the contrary, the thought of our close attachment to *El*, God, will inspire each child of Israel to walk in the path of goodness, righteousness, and truth.